I0051917

LEADERTHINK ®

Inspiring Reminders to Think – and Act – Like a Leader

Tracy Brown

Dallas, Texas
2009

LeaderThink®
Inspiring Reminders to Think – and Act – Like a Leader
Volume 1
By Tracy Brown

©2009
All rights reserved. No part of this book may be used or reproduced in any manner whatsoever, including Internet usage, without written permission from the author.

ISBN-13: 978-1-889819-24-2

Cover design by www.kbiDesigns.com
Author Photo: Jim Duncan, www.DuncanPhotography.com

brown bridges books
PO Box 12866
Dallas TX 75225

In Appreciation

To the many leaders who have been role models for me. Thank you for helping me experience so many different leadership styles in so many different settings. I am grateful to have this opportunity to share what I have learned with the readers of this book.

Other Books by This Author

Author:

LeaderThink®: Inspiring Reminders to Think – and Act – Like a Leader, Volume 2

Breaking the Barrier of Bias: The Subtle Influence of Bias and What to Do About It.

71 Ways to Demonstrate Commitment to Diversity

motiVersity: Motivating While Valuing Diversity

Diagnosis Diversity: How to Maximize Diversity in Healthcare Settings

Contributing Author:

The Productivity Path: Your Roadmap for Improving Employee Performance!

The Leadership Path: Your Roadmap for Leading People in the 21st Century!

The Service Path: Your Roadmap for Building Strong Customer Loyalty!

Affiliated Websites

www.TheWayLeadersThink.com
www.DiversityTrends.com
www.TracyBrown.com
www.DiagnosisDiversity.com
www.DiversityResourcesonSale.com
www.DiversityAwarenessWeek.com

LeaderThink®

Inspiring Reminders to Think – and Act – Like a Leader

Welcome!

There are (at least) three ways to use this book.

1. A few of you will read this book in sequence. You will enjoy the variety of quotations and the commentaries in pretty much the same sequence as they were written for the email newsletter.

2. Most of you will scan the Table of Contents to find a quote that interests you or addresses a current concern. Then you can go to the corresponding page and read the commentary related to the quotation you selected.

3. And some of you will just open the book to a random page and see what ideas or insights are there. This is a great strategy when you just want to energize your practice of leadership and you're not facing any specific challenge.

If you are new to LeaderThink® this book gives you the opportunity to read and enjoy messages from the past. Since the weekly series provides new quotations and commentaries each week, new subscribers are often curious about previous messages.

If you are already a subscriber to the LeaderThink® weekly series you'll appreciate the convenience of having so many of the previous messages all in one document for easy reference.

This book won't turn you into the best leader in the world in 10 simple steps. But each time you pick it up it will remind you that you can be a great leader. It will provide bite-size reminders you can read in five minutes or less to stay encouraged. It will help you remember it's up to you to think, and act, like a leader!

Table of Contents

LeaderThink®...v

"Leadership is action, not position."..1

"If you waste your life sitting on the fence, you'll end up going nowhere in the brief time you have left."..2

"Within our dreams and aspirations we find our opportunities."....................3

"A good leader is not the person who does things right, but the person who finds the right things to do."..5

"No individual has any right to come into the world and go out of it without leaving behind."...7

"You know that you can't really make much of a difference in things until you change yourself."..9

"Good leaders make people feel that they're at the very heart of things, not at the periphery. Everyone feels that he or she makes a difference to the success of the organization. When that happens, people feel centered and that gives their work meaning."..11

"Words mean nothing. Action is the only thing. Doing; that's the only thing."...............13

"What success I achieved in the theater is due to the fact that I have always worked just as hard when there were ten people in the house as when there were thousands. Just as hard in Springfield, Illinois as on Broadway."..15

"Management that wants to change an institution must first show it loves that institution."..17

"A person wrapped up in himself makes a very small package."........................19

"If I'd known I was going to live this long, I'd have taken better care of myself."............21

"Before you speak, ask yourself: Is it kind, is it necessary, is it true, does it improve on the silence?"..23

"Impossibilities are merely things of which we have not learned, or which we do not wish to happen."...24

The difference between a boss and leader: A boss says, "Go!" A leader says, "Let's go!" 25

"Those who profess to favor freedom, and yet depreciate agitation, are men who want crops without plowing up the ground." 27

"We cannot solve our problems with the same level of thinking that created them." 28

"Instead of making others right or wrong, or bottling up right and wrong in ourselves, there's a middle way, a very powerful middle way. Could we have no agenda when we walk into a room with another person; not know what to say; not make that person wrong or right? Could we see, hear, feel other people as they really are? It is powerful to practice this way. True communication can happen only in that open space." 29

"Even if you think you're on the right track, you'll get run over if you just sit there." 31

"The price one pays for pursuing any profession, or calling, is an intimate knowledge of its ugly side." 33

"Transition failures happen when new leaders either misunderstand the essential demands of the situation or lack the skill and flexibility to adapt to them." 35

"A brand (or a new product offering) is nothing more than an idea. Ideas that spread are more likely to succeed than those that don't." 37

"None of us is responsible for the complexion of his skin. This fact of nature offers no clue to the character or quality of the person underneath." 38

"You can't look forward and backward at the same time." 39

"Never work just for money or for power. They won't save your soul or help you sleep at night." 41

"Sometimes you got to hurt something to help something. Sometimes you have to plow under one thing in order for something else to grow." 43

"Objectives are not fate; they are direction. They are not commands; they are commitments. They do not determine the future; they are means to mobilize the resources and energies of the business for the making of the future." 45

"Peak performers concentrate on solving problems rather than placing blame for them." 47

"What the people want is very simple. They want an America as good as its promise." 49

"It is amazing what you can accomplish if you do not care who gets the credit." 50

"Recognize the story you make up is your own." 51

"If the rate of change on the outside exceeds the rate of change on the inside, the end is near." 53

"A word to the wise ain't necessary -- it's the stupid ones who need advice." 54

"Leadership is the capacity to translate vision into reality." 55

"Unless we look the beast in the eye we find it has an uncanny habit of returning to hold us hostage." 56

"Leadership is the ability to hide your panic from others." 57

"It is commitment, not authority, which produces results." 59

"Discomfort from confrontation can provide great growth. If you're not experiencing any resistance, you're not moving forward." 61

"Time is neutral. It can be used either destructively or constructively." 63

"If you always do what you always did, you will always get what you always got." 65

"If you don't like where you are in life, there comes a point when you must give up the part of you that's keeping you back." 67

"Think of it as evolution instead of failure." 69

Everyone yearns for a better life. Yet few people take even the smallest steps in that direction." 71

"Words can hurt and words can heal. What did your words do today?" 73

"Instead of changing addresses, address the issue." 74

"Like a rubber ball, the harder you get thrown down signifies the higher you'll rise when you bounce back" 75

"You must genuinely like and respect those who are performing under your command, for neither the liking nor the respect can be successfully faked." 77

"I used to want the words "She tried" on my tombstone. Now I want "She did it." 79

"The most dangerous leadership myth is that leaders are born—that there is a genetic factor to leadership. This myth asserts that people simply either have certain charismatic qualities or not. That's nonsense; in fact, the opposite is true. Leaders are made rather than born." 81

"An organization with an indispensable man is guilty of management failure." 83

"Who is Robert - and why do we still follow his rules anyway?" 85

"Being given a particular organizational title may confer some hierarchical authority, but it certainly does not make you a leader."..87

"Good leaders make others good leaders."..89

"Every company has two organizational structures: the formal one is written on the charts; the other is the living relationship of the men and women in the organization."...90

"Come out from behind yourself into the conversation and make it real."....................91

"Why are you so afraid to say what is true for you? Do you think I can not handle your truth? Or do you think I can not handle the ways we differ?"..................................93

"The ultimate measure of a man is not where he stands in moments of comfort and convenience, but where he stands in times of challenge and controversy."...................95

"I have a great belief in the fact that whenever there is chaos, it creates wonderful thinking. I consider chaos a gift."..97

"Fear is the single greatest obstacle to success"..99

"When you find a man who has lost his way, you don't make fun of him and scorn him and leave him there. You show him the way. If you don't do that you just prove that you're sort of lost yourself."..100

"It is only those who are free inside who can help those around them."......................101

"Everybody has barriers and obstacles. If you look at them as containing fences that don't allow you to advance, then you're going to be a failure. If you look at them as hurdles that strengthen you each time you go over one, then you're going to be a success."..103

"I have no mercy or compassion in me for a society that will crush people and then penalize them for not being able to stand up under the weight."..................................105

"XPS M2010: Ultimate Innovation."..107

"An adventure is only an inconvenience, rightly considered."...................................109

"When we turn our backs on feelings we should deal with, they fester and grow and ultimately consume us. Silence is denial. Silence is anxiety."....................................111

"If you understood everything I say, you'd be me."..113

"Lots of times you have to pretend to join a parade in which you're not really interested in order to get where you're going."..115

"Fear is the energy to do your best in a new situation. The feeling of fear is really preparation energy. It's getting you ready to excel, to succeed, to do your best and to learn the most." 117

"Losers visualize the penalties of failure. Winners visualize the rewards of success." 118

"The best way to escape from a problem is to solve it." 121

"If you don't have confidence, you'll always find a way not to win." 123

"He not busy being born is busy dying." 124

"The inferior teacher tells you that something is wrong with you and offers to fix it. The superior teacher tells you that something is right with you and helps you bring it forth." 125

"Let your life speak." 127

"Are you a leader because you want to receive the recognition, admiration and respect of others? Or are you a leader because the respect, admiration and respect of others has placed you in a position to lead?" 129

"Courage is the atom of change." 131

"The weirdest thing most of us do is avoid the very people we need to be around." 133

"Don't let yesterday use up too much of today." 135

"Everything will change. The only question is growing up or decaying." 137

"He who chatters with you will chatter of you." 139

"The greatest threat to freedom is the absence of criticism." 140

"There is no such thing as a 'natural'. A natural dancer has to practice hard. A natural painter has to paint all the time. And a natural fool has to work at it." 141

"Character, not circumstances, makes the man." 143

"Self-discipline, as a virtue or as an acquired asset, can be valuable to anyone." 145

Some Closing Thoughts 146

About Tracy Brown 147

"*Leadership is action, not position.*"

Donald H. McGannon

Isn't that true?

Regardless of their title, the leaders we most admire didn't just talk about change or improvement or success. They took action that helped their organization implement change, demonstrate improvement or achieve success.

We all know people who had great titles, but we didn't consider them leaders because their actions didn't inspire us, improve the organization or demonstrate commitment to key stakeholders.

So, this week, remember your title means nothing without appropriate action that communicates to others your commitment, your compassion and your courage.

Commit to take action on at least one thing you've been talking about doing for a long time. Just take one step forward. Now!

Think . . . and act . . . like a leader!

"If you waste your life sitting on the fence, you'll end up going nowhere in the brief time you have left."
Bradley Trevor Greive

I am a strong advocate for doing your homework, getting solid information and learning from mistakes made by others. But there comes a point when you just have to make a decision and move forward.

It's hard to commit to a course of action when you aren't absolutely sure it's the right decision. But good leaders know that after collecting a certain amount of data a decision must be made.

When our leaders fail to make decision and take action, the entire organization loses momentum. So, stop "sitting on the fence" any longer than necessary. Gather data and develop an action plan. Communicate the plan and move forward.

Great leaders know a plan can be revised mid-stream if it's not working. But you'll never know if it will work until you get off the fence and start implementation!

Think . . . and act . . . like a leader!

"Within our dreams and aspirations we find our opportunities."
Sugar Ray Leonard

If you want to recognize an opportunity that is right in front of you, you must know what you are trying to achieve.

Our visions of success, and the goals we set, are our dreams for the future.

The people we meet and the information we learn can open the door to success if we have established clear goals.

Are you a leader with a clear vision?

What are your dreams for your team or organization?

If you can't answer those questions with passion and excitement let me suggest that you take the time, this week, to clarify where you want to be a year from now.

Once you've have the future clearly in mind you will begin to recognize the opportunities that are within your reach today.

These opportunities are like stepping stones leading you closer toward your goals.

Think . . . and act . . . like a leader!

"A good leader is not the person who does things right, but the person who finds the right things to do."

Anthony T. Dadovano

Afraid to take a chance?

Trying to be perfect?

Stuck in the paralysis of analysis?

Leaders listen to their key stakeholders, do research, consider the options, and then take a measured risk. Perfection is not always possible. But progress is the result of carefully choosing the next step based on the information available at the time the decision is made.

How do you know what "the right things" are? If you can answer the questions below with a "Yes!" then it might be the right thing.

- Is there a direct link between this and our mission?
- Will this immediately address challenges or issues shared by our employees, customers or members?

- Does it provide a value-added benefit to a key stakeholder group?
- Is it something I don't want to do, but almost everyone else believes it's the right next step?
- Do we have the research that indicates this will work, but I just want to test it one or two more times to be sure?

How do you know what "the wrong things" are?

- I want to do because it will make me look good but it doesn't really bring a tangible benefit to the team or the organization.
- It makes sense to me, but just about everybody else questions it or says it won't work.
- It addresses a future (anticipated) issue that is less important than the immediate issues people are complaining about.
- If we implement this it will create excessive friction among team members or departments (creating a new problem bigger than the one I'm trying to solve.)

This week, stop trying to get everything right. Instead, strive to do the right things. If you do enough right things, people will forgive you when you occasionally drop the ball or make a mistake.

Think . . . and act . . . like a leader!

"No individual has any right to come into the world and go out of it without leaving behind."

George Washington Carver

If I interviewed 10 people who worked with you what would they tell me you were "leaving behind?" Just what is the legacy created by your leadership?

Saying, "I want to make this organization better." is not enough. What specific programs or activities or improvements are you creating, implementing and nurturing?

It may be okay with you that people simply remember you as a nice person. Don't get me wrong . . . being remembered as someone who was nice to others is a great (and difficult) accomplishment. But you were not hired, elected or placed in your current leadership role just to be nice!

You are a leader who can influence the progress (or lack of progress) your group makes toward achieving its goals. It is your leadership legacy that will close the gap between today's reality and your organization's vision.

This week, I challenge you to choose one thing you want to leave behind when you retire, are promoted or leave your elected position. Then draft a strategy for achieving that goal.

If it makes a positive difference in the life of another person or in the success of your organization, it will make a positive statement about the legacy of your life as a leader.

Think . . . and act . . . like a leader!

"You know that you can't really make much of a difference in things until you change yourself."
Alice Walker

"Ouch!" You mean I need to stop talking about all the things everybody else is doing wrong and just focus on doing my best?

Gee, that's not nearly as much fun and pointing fingers at others.

It's easy for us to see what's wrong with our department. And we can point out the problems in our organization with little hesitation.

What we often forget is that if we are a part of the system, then we have contributed, in some way, to those problems existing or continuing.

So rather than point our finger at others, we should figure out what we can do to generate a different outcome in the future and be willing to change in order to be part of the solution.

This week, choose one thing you will do differently, think about differently or communicate differently. Change yourself and you'll be surprised how quickly others follow your lead!

Think . . . and act . . . like a leader!

"Good leaders make people feel that they're at the very heart of things, not at the periphery. Everyone feels that he or she makes a difference to the success of the organization. When that happens, people feel centered and that gives their work meaning."

Warren Bennis

Cheerleading provided me with a great experience for learning to be a leader among peers, since all of us were volunteers and none of us could terminate the others. We were judged based on our team performance just as often as we were noticed for our individual skills and talents. As captain of the varsity squad, I was the elected leader, but my success was based on the passion, productivity and performance of the group.

Since then, I've been in many positions where I had the authority to get things done, to tell people what to do and to use my personal power or skills to achieve established goals. But some of my best successes have been when the other people involved felt like they were a valued part of the decision-making process and an essential part of the solution.

This is not about people liking you, or feeling that you are their friend. When I was a cheerleading captain there were dozens of times I had to enforce rules and make unpopular decisions. Friendship is not as important as fairness. A great leader demonstrates on a regular basis that s/he knows, and values, the talents and skills others bring to the tasks the team or organization must accomplish.

So, next time you criticize or correct someone on your team, ask yourself, "When is the last time I told this person what I believe to be the ways s/he contributes to this team's success?"

This week pick a couple of people you need to improve your relationship with. Say thank you for their contributions in the past. Share what you see as their strengths and talents. Solicit their suggestions about ways you or the team can improve. And find out how you can help him or her contribute even more to your team or organization in the future.

Think . . . and act . . . like a leader!

"Words mean nothing. Action is the only thing. Doing; that's the only thing."

Ernest J Gaines

It is so easy to send out an email message promising great change. And it's almost as easy to stand in front of a group and give a great speech about the future. The hard work is translating those words into actions.

Great leaders are not afraid to promise things they are not quite sure they can achieve. That happens all the times when you set goals that will stretch you or your organization beyond your current capabilities. But in that kind of situation the leader is demonstrating every day his or her commitment to achieving that goal. They are communicating constantly, involving team members, providing resources and otherwise showing they are actively engaged in working toward the stated goal.

It is through their actions that great leaders make it clear that they believe in the organization and that their commitment is solid.

Don't be a leader who says the right things but then does nothing to help guide the organization toward success.

Think . . . and act . . . like a leader!

"What success I achieved in the theater is due to the fact that I have always worked just as hard when there were ten people in the house as when there were thousands. Just as hard in Springfield, Illinois as on Broadway."

Bill "Bojangles" Robinson

Your parents or other adult mentor probably told you, "Always do your best."

It's sometimes tempting to be less attentive or less responsive to the people we think of as less influential or less powerful. But when you are a leader, every person you interact with can affect the success, or failure, of your organization or team.

The person you give less than your best to might be the one person who can connect you to the sponsor or buyer you've been trying to reach for months. Or the person you are slow to respond to could have just the right experience to solve a problem your team has been facing. Or, he or she could be interviewed by a reporter the next week and asked about your organization.

Set your standards high, and then apply those standards as consistently as you can with everyone you meet.

Think . . . and act . . . like a leader!

"Management that wants to change an institution must first show it loves that institution."

John Tusa

New employee. First day of work. In less than four hours he has criticized five programs and insulted half the people he's met. What's his likelihood of being accepted warmly by his new peers?

Obviously we all know better. Even if his new peers agree with him, they will be wary of this newcomer, who doesn't know how things are done around here and who is brash enough (or stupid enough) to vocalize these opinions. Few people would risk their own success by becoming fast allies with this opinionated newcomer.

So why do so many of us, when we step into leadership positions, act as if everyone who came before us was ignorant, inept and irresponsible?

Even if the leader you are replacing did not do a good job, criticism of that leader might also be interpreted as criticism of the people who worked with that leader. There is more to be gained from praising the things that have been done well in the past and by focusing on the mission of the organization.

Hold your criticism of the past and demonstrate your respect for the people you are working with now. Engage people in conversations that result in a shared vision of the future.

When people can see how much you are committed to the future success of the organization, they can then begin to believe you are also committed to their success as individuals.

Think . . . and act . . . like a leader!

"A person wrapped up in himself makes a very small package."

Denzel Washington

You've worked hard and you've been successful.

You have talents and skills that make you stand out from the crowd.

You are pretty special -- and not just because your mother, your life partner, or your best friend thinks so.

You are a great leader.

Great leaders remember leadership comes with a responsibility to serve. Leaders are being relied upon to make a positive difference for others. Leaders are expected to generate results for the organizations they work within.

Leaders are like symphony conductors pulling the best from each musician and weaving it together to create a musical masterpiece.

A leader whose primary motivation is self-glory usually doesn't lead for long. Without a clear focus on serving others or on creating a significant benefit for the organization, a leader has no charge.

This week, remind yourself that it's not about you.

Think . . . and act . . . like a leader!

"If I'd known I was going to live this long, I'd have taken better care of myself."
Eubie Blake

Are you one of those leaders who is so busy doing everything that you neglect your health or your family?

Don't make the mistake of thinking there will always be time next month, next year or after you retire.

Take care of yourself now.

This week notice what percentage of your time you spend exercising, sharing positive experiences with family members or friends and doing fun things with those you care about.

Also notice what percentage of your time you spend with people you don't enjoy or time spent complaining about how much work you have and the deadlines you are facing.

Finally, notice what percentage of the food you eat is healthy and nourishing, compared to the percentage of food you eat that you know is not good for you.

Choose to take care of yourself. Choose to surround yourself as often as possible with people you love, respect or enjoy. Let me remind you that you can only be a great leader making a positive difference if you are alive and well.

Think . . . and act . . . like a leader!

"Before you speak, ask yourself: Is it kind, is it necessary, is it true, does it improve on the silence?"
Shirdi Sai Baba

Great leaders know there are times to be quiet. There are times to let others speak and to simply listen. Take it in. Think about it.

Don't think that just because you are the leader you should always have the answers. Don't insist on always having the last word.

Instead, sometimes just invite others to share their ideas and opinions without judgment or decisions being made.

Even when you have a strong opinion or a major disagreement, you can sometimes benefit from asking yourself, "Is this the best time to bring this up?"

Think . . . and act . . . like a leader!

"Impossibilities are merely things of which we have not learned, or which we do not wish to happen."
Charles W Chesnutt

I once reported to a man who believed he was so smart and so well-read that if he didn't know about something it didn't exist.

That sounds pretty arrogant, but think about yourself as a leader. You've been quite successful and you do know a lot about your areas of expertise. When people suggest things you've already decided aren't good solutions how do you handle that?

I wonder if you too come across as if you believe you are such an expert that your perception about the potential of another person's idea must be the correct and best view.

As leaders we must all struggle with walking the fine line between expert and experimenter. Experimentation is necessary for our organizations, and the people in them, to grow.

Think . . . and act . . . like a leader!

The difference between a boss and leader: A boss says, "Go!" A leader says, "Let's go!"
Source Unknown

I think it is very possible to be a good boss and not be a good leader. Most of us have experienced a number of good bosses throughout our adult life, but only a small percentage of them were people we would also describe as fabulous leaders!

The good boss is someone you don't mind working for. She is a nice person who assigns tasks and responsibilities and sends people off to do what they are expected to do.

The good boss is someone you don't mind giving a card to when Bosses Day is celebrated each October. He is effective, fair and respected and he often has an outstanding track record of achievement.

But being a boss AND a leader means that people who report to you feel they are working WITH you to achieve a goal instead of FOR you.

Being a boss AND a leader means that people look forward to working with you -- even when the task or responsibility is something they aren't excited about doing. People want to work with leaders they can trust, leaders they can learn from and leaders who inspire them to do their best work.

There are different ways to achieve this. And different situations require different approaches. But the key is, in my opinion, continuously asking: "What can I do this month to include others, honor the contributions of others, learn from others and build long-term relationships?"

Think . . . and act . . . like a leader!

"Those who profess to favor freedom, and yet depreciate agitation, are men who want crops without plowing up the ground."
Frederick Douglass

It is impossible to lead an organization through change without people going through discomfort, fear, anger, depression and a little bit of insanity.

As leaders, it is our job to "plow the ground" with purpose. We must help people understand why change is needed; and what benefits they can expect in the future. If you want to be a part of the team that takes your organization to the next level of success, but you are afraid of the controversy and chaos that is a natural part of change, you have some work to do on yourself before you can lead others.

This week, accept your responsibility for stirring up a little controversy in order to improve your organization. And if you need assistance to become more comfortable leading in times of change seek out a mentor, coach or class to help you develop the skills you need.

Think . . . and act . . . like a leader!

"We cannot solve our problems with the same level of thinking that created them."
Albert Einstein

Bring in some fresh thinkers if you keep tackling the same problems with the same solutions. Or, create a team experience that forces you to begin to think on a different level or from a different approach.

If you don't do something to change the pool of ideas, you'll never take your team or organization to the next level.

There are dozens of ways to invite input or feedback from your customers or other key stakeholders. You can also form a committee or task force and invite people with a fresh perspective to participate in problem-solving discussions.

The key is to acknowledge the stale thinking and to take action that initiates a fresh approach and new alternatives.

Think . . . and act . . . like a leader!

"Instead of making others right or wrong, or bottling up right and wrong in ourselves, there's a middle way, a very powerful middle way. Could we have no agenda when we walk into a room with another person; not know what to say; not make that person wrong or right? Could we see, hear, feel other people as they really are? It is powerful to practice this way. True communication can happen only in that open space."

Pema Chodron

It's so hard sometimes to remember everybody is doing the best they can based on what they know or what they have experienced in the past.

Often we walk into meetings so sure of our own agenda that we hear any comment that questions our thoughts as a personal attack. What would happen if we instead just heard the question as an attempt to understand?

Or what if we thought of the person who criticized our idea as a really good friend who also wants the best for our organization, but simply has a different view?

This week, check yourself when you find yourself thinking of another person as your enemy or as a barrier to your vision of success.

Challenge yourself to hear criticism and disagreement as a gift of feedback you would never hear from those who think exactly the way you think.

Calm your anger and practice patience with those who have an approach different from yours. Instead of attacking their thoughts and ideas, ask questions and offer alternatives. Be honest, but also be respectful.

Keeping the lines of communication open is one of the leader's most valuable tools. Accepting, and giving, negative feedback is a difficult skill to master. The first step is managing our own behavior.

Think . . . and act . . . like a leader!

"Even if you think you're on the right track, you'll get run over if you just sit there."

Will Rogers

Do you know this person?

She has great ideas. She knows what needs to be done. She knows how to do it. But weeks or months go by and she hasn't made any progress toward the goal.

Sometimes it's procrastination that keeps us from acting.

Sometimes we're overwhelmed because we've committed to too many high priority tasks.

But often we just slow down once we know what we need to do because we feel as if we have solved the problem.

When we fail to implement the solution our organization experiences no benefit. Just because we can tell people what needs to be done doesn't resolve the problem.

While we are thinking about our great solution, another organization will meet the needs of our customers; employees will leave and go work for the competition; or our members will ignore requests to renew.

This week, select one thing you will implement within the next 14 days.

Think . . . and act . . . like a leader!

"The price one pays for pursuing any profession, or calling, is an intimate knowledge of its ugly side."

James Baldwin

Most of us came into leadership pretty idealistic. We wanted to make a difference. We were creative or smart or lucky. We anticipated some challenges, but for the most part we were excited about being recognized as a leader.

What we didn't realize was that in order to lead we'd also get to know all the problems that need to be fixed. We didn't realize that in order to make a real difference we would be challenged with all the "behind the scenes" politics and positioning that goes on in organizations. We could never have imagined the range of predicaments we would face as a leader!

But great leaders are sometimes like The Wizard of Oz. We must hold up the best of our world to the public, giving them hope and faith and security; while we frantically work behind the curtain with limited tools, limited skills and limited resources. Leaders make magic from the most mundane resources.

To make the best impact we must hear, and welcome, the worst in our organizations to come before us. Only then can we create programs, activities and services that meet the real needs of our primary stakeholders.

And don't forget . . . often those who rely on us for guidance have the answers themselves. It's our job, as leaders, to help others recognize, and trust, their own potential.

Don't be agitated by the 'difficult people' or the 'dirty laundry' in your organization. Instead remember that this is the part of the organization only a few leaders are privileged to see.

Think . . . and act . . . like a leader!

"Transition failures happen when new leaders either misunderstand the essential demands of the situation or lack the skill and flexibility to adapt to them."

Michael Watkins

Maybe you have worked in a company where a specific position experienced great turnover through three or four consecutive managers in a short period of time. When each of the managers was selected everyone was convinced this was the leader who could turn that department or organization around. Yet one by one, each failed or left before achieving much progress.

We might have excellent skills and great knowledge; but if we work on the symptoms instead of the cause the problem will still prevail.

If we have great talent and experience, but our areas of expertise don't apply to the challenge before us, we may not be able to improve the situation.

So, as leaders, we must be careful to assess each leadership challenge objectively. And we must be willing to engage the right people to help us correct the problems we face.

Think you can do no wrong? Get over it!

Think you can do it by yourself? Get real!

The best leaders are brutally honest with themselves, and others, about the skills they have and the areas where they need help.

Think . . . and act . . . like a leader

"A brand (or a new product offering) is nothing more than an idea. Ideas that spread are more likely to succeed than those that don't."

Seth Godin

No matter how great your ideas are if people don't get excited about them, they aren't going to succeed.

How effectively do you communicate your ideas? Do you use language that others can easily remember and repeat to others?

This week take at least three concepts that are critical to your team's success and identify the core idea behind each one. Develop a one-sentence description of the benefit each program or activity has. Then test your language with at least five different people.

The real test? Call or email them next week and see what they can remember or repeat.

Think . . . and act . . . like a leader.

"None of us is responsible for the complexion of his skin. This fact of nature offers no clue to the character or quality of the person underneath."
Marian Anderson

Periodically we need a reminder that we don't know everything about others we work with just by looking at the outer package. All of us sometimes forget that our stereotypes about other people are stories we've made up in our minds about what others can and can't do.

None of us want to be judged by how we look. We want to have a fair opportunity to use all our skills and talents to help our organizations achieve success.

This week, pay attention to your evaluation of people. Is it based on what people have actually done or said? Or is your opinion based on what you believe might be true based on that person's ethnicity, gender, religion, age, education, etc.?

Give people a chance to surprise you.

Think . . . and act . . . like a leader.

"You can't look forward and backward at the same time."

Coleman Young

It's time to let go of all the problems people caused in the past.

You are a leader for today and tomorrow. Your charge is to help create a successful future.

I admit it's difficult sometimes to stay focused on the future when you've been brought in to fix problems that have existed for a long time. But once you understand the problems you should be helping everyone focus on the future.

This does not mean you ignore the past.

On the contrary, one of your first responsibilities is to get as much information as you can about what has been done, and not done, and why. It's very important to know what was successful and what failures occurred in the past.

But once you've acquired that information and used it to identify the most important current strategies, you have to stop looking backwards and focus on the future.

You can't change the past. Your organization is depending on you to shape the future.

Think . . . and act . . . like a leader.

"Never work just for money or for power. They won't save your soul or help you sleep at night."
Marian Wright Edelman

What is the joy you get from your work?

If you were told you must stay in your current job (or current volunteer leader role) but exactly 365 days from now you would die in your sleep, would that change the way you work? What would you do differently? How would you change your life?

If you knew you had only one year to live, would you continue to work the way you do, doing the same things with the same people for the same reasons?

This week, remember the real reason you get up and go to work each day. Or the real reason you spend so much time being a leader in a professional association or community organization.

If the number one reason is for a paycheck you may be making a lot of money but you are missing the joy of life.

Your life's labor deserves your best. Choose what you want your leadership legacy to be and begin, this week, living and leading, from joy.

Think . . . and act . . . like a leader!

"Sometimes you got to hurt something to help something. Sometimes you have to plow under one thing in order for something else to grow."
Ernest J Gaines

What worked five years ago simply may not be the best solution for today's situation.

As leaders, we are sometimes required to end a program, activity, process, or a relationship with a client or organization we love.

We may have even been a part of creating this program and we know all the history. Still, if it does not serve the organization now, it has to go (or be improved or changed in some significant way).

Leaders live in the present.

Extraordinary leaders prepare their organizations for the future.

Sometimes that requires the ability to say goodbye.

This week, honor the traditions of your organization, but also look with a leader's eye at the programs and activities that exist. Are there changes that need to be made? How will you, as a leader, help your team honor history but also create the future?

Think . . . and act . . . like a leader!

"Objectives are not fate; they are direction. They are not commands; they are commitments. They do not determine the future; they are means to mobilize the resources and energies of the business for the making of the future."

Peter Drucker

Pass/Fail. Complete/Incomplete. All too often we think of the objectives we establish as the only possible end result. And we judge ourselves based on whether or not we achieved those objectives. And as a leader we usually have a clear vision of exactly what steps it will take to meet each objective.

What would be different for you if you instead viewed your objectives as important and valuable, but simply the end result of many decisions, many actions and much progress along the way?

As we progress toward our objectives we often learn new information or meet new people or identify alternate options that change our path. Shouldn't we recognize and value these course corrections?

And as leaders, the more people we involve in order to achieve these objectives, the more likely it is that there will be people who want to take a different path to achieve the agreed-upon objectives. Are you comfortable with diversity in work style, thinking style and execution?

This week focus on clearly stating your objectives and noticing the many different ways those objectives might be met!

Think . . . and act . . . like a leader!

"Peak performers concentrate on solving problems rather than placing blame for them."
Charles Garfield

Whether the issue you are facing is a major natural disaster, or a missed deadline on a monthly report, the need is the same. Focus on fixing the root cause and the system that produced the unwanted result. Do not focus on who did what to screw up!

Now this doesn't mean you never correct people. The ability to give constructive criticism and coaching feedback is a skill all good leaders should develop. However, getting to the root of a problem requires more than focusing on who is to blame for whatever error has occurred.

If you believe a problem will never occur again because you've punished or trained the individual(s) who were at fault you will face bigger problems down the line.

Look deeper at the systems in place to orient and develop staff. Consider whether the communications systems currently used insure proactive response to potential problems. And what systems exist to fix problems once they occur?

Blaming others doesn't get you off the hook as a leader. Great leaders look deeper and focus on solving the root cause of problems that occur.

Think . . . and act . . . like a leader!

"What the people want is very simple. They want an America as good as its promise."
Barbara Jordan

Adaptation #1:
What the people in your organization want is very simple. They want an organization as good as the one you have promised them. Everyday.

Adaptation #2:
What your customers want is very simple. They want a product or service as good as the one you promised them. Every time.

Adaptation #3:
What your family wants is very simple. They want you to be a person as good as the one you promised them. Forever.

Leaders make promises to help create a desired future state. Great leaders consistently fulfill their promises.

Think . . . and act . . . like a leader!

"It is amazing what you can accomplish if you do not care who gets the credit."
Harry S Truman

One of the most common complaints employees have is that their boss takes credit for their work. One of the biggest barriers to volunteer involvement in nonprofits is that the work of volunteers goes unacknowledged.

Credit must be given to those who do the work required to accomplish the goals of your organization. As a leader you are ultimately responsible for attaining goals, but there is no way you can do that alone.

Do the people who work with you feel you take credit for their contributions? Is their only sense of success indirectly attained?

Find ways to recognize and publicize the work of others and watch the commitment and productivity of your team improve!

Think . . . and act . . . like a leader!

"Recognize the story you make up is your own."
Tracy Brown

What you really know, or understand, about any other person is limited. Most of what you think you know about others is a story you made up about them.

Based on what people say or do in our presence we make up a story about who they are, whether or not we trust them, whether or not we like them and whether or not we want to work with them.

As leaders it is important to slow down our judgment of others in order to engage a wider variety of people. Great leaders have the ability to value many different types of people who demonstrate a wide range of values and experiences.

When I find myself having difficulty connecting with a colleague or customer I remind myself, "The story I am making up about this person may, or may not be true. It is a story based on my values, my priorities and my past experiences, not theirs."

Then I challenge myself to ask a question or to request specific behavior that can build a more effective connection with this person.

The key to making the questions work is to ask questions that are designed to help you understand the other person better. Questions that challenge the other person's values, beliefs or behavior are less effective because that only puts him or her on the defensive.

The second key to making this work is to make requests that describe specific behavior you know will result in better communication or improved trust from your perspective. You must also be open to the other person saying your request is unreasonable or impossible to achieve. (In other words you are making a request, not delivering an order!)

This week, evaluate whether the stories you have made up about people you are uncomfortable with are their stories or yours. And remember . . . everyone you interact with is making up their story about you!

Think . . . and act . . . like a leader

"If the rate of change on the outside exceeds the rate of change on the inside, the end is near."
Jack Welch

Sometimes our own success can hurt us. If we have experienced great success it's hard to understand why, and how, we must change.

But as the external environment responds to changing demographics, new technology, shifting expectations of our key stakeholders and other influences, it becomes necessary to update our internal systems and processes. We must look at the products and services we offer and assess whether it's time to make some changes.

This week, take a deep look at the way your team or organization responds to change. Choose to be a voice for improvement.

Think . . . and act . . . like a leader!

"A word to the wise ain't necessary -- it's the stupid ones who need advice."
Fat Albert's Survival Kit (Bill Cosby)

If you are like me, you often find yourself "preaching to the choir" or talking with people who already agree with your message or opinion.

There is nothing wrong with that; however it is important to share your wisdom with those who are making mistakes because they have not been exposed to the same information as you.

When your insights can help someone improve his life it does no good to complain to everyone around him, but never talk directly to him. When your experience can help someone become a stronger contributor, it does no good to judge her weaknesses without providing tips and tools to help her develop stronger skills.

Great leaders keep their eyes open for opportunities to coach others in a proactive way.

Think . . . and act . . . like a leader!

"Leadership is the capacity to translate vision into reality."

Warren G. Bennis

Having a great vision for your organization does not make you a leader. It just makes you a visionary.

Knowing, in your head, what needs to happen to turn a struggling organization around does not make you a leader. It just makes you an idea-person.

Believing in the potential of your organization does not make you a leader. It just makes you a passionate supporter.

What makes you a leader is when you have a clear vision, an understanding of strategy and strong passion COMBINED with consistent and measurable action that marshals the resources required to effect change and inspire people.

Think . . . and act . . . like a leader!

"Unless we look the beast in the eye we find it has an uncanny habit of returning to hold us hostage."
Bishop Desmund Tutu

As leaders it's important for us to create an environment that encourages healthy confrontation of difficult issues.

If we let our fear of confrontation bury the tough issues that exist in the organizations we lead we are not fulfilling our responsibility to lead.

Conflict ignored does not go away; it just goes underground. And when it does erupt, the entire foundation of your leadership success is at risk.

So be courageous, but also be prepared. Make sure you learn, and practice, conflict resolution skills. Develop your ability to participate in dialogue about difficult or sensitive topics. Always have a list of skilled facilitators you know and trust; bring one of them in to lead difficult conversations you are not sure you can handle.

Think . . . and act . . . like a leader.

"Leadership is the ability to hide your panic from others."

Rabbi Dr. Edwin H. Friedman

I love, love, love this quote! So many times I've wondered, "Why do they think I know the answer to this problem?" or "What on earth am I going to do to get beyond this barrier?"

When you are a leader, people expect you to guide the organization around, over or through all kinds of issues. Most of the time we find ourselves in leadership roles because we have a track record of resolving issues and developing successful strategies, but when faced with a new problem, an unexpected question or a situation that has never existed before we panic just like everybody else!

As a teenager I was put into a variety of leadership roles. I often felt ill-equipped to deal with the people issues involved in leading a team. But because I was a good listener I quickly learned that asking questions often resulted in either the problem resolving itself or the people around me developing a great solution.

As I have matured as a leader I find that I don't so much "hide" my panic from others as much as I "delay" the panic long enough to assess the situation.

I notice my initial panic reaction and a voice in my head says, "Ok, before you panic, find out what's really going on." Or that same little voice says, "Uh-oh. This is a new one. Ask more questions before you jump to conclusions." And then, if I still feel a sense of panic the little voice whispers, "Who do you know who can help you with this?"

This is the little voice that makes the panic get in line behind great listening, calm thinking and asking for help.

As a leader you can never be in control of every little thing. And all the mundane, easy-to-resolve issues should be handled by others in your organization. So if something has escalated to you, it's natural to feel a little panic when faced with those out-of-control, super-sized challenges.

Recognize your first reaction of panic, then take a deep breath and look for creative, effective options for action.

Think . . . and act . . . like a leader!

"It is commitment, not authority, which produces results."

William Gore

There is position power. You are someone's boss and they do what you tell them to. You have authority and people follow your direction. Things get done, but people may not be committed to the project or the organization.

When people do things only because you tell them to, their commitment is not as deep.

Leaders in non-profit organizations and community activities often work with volunteers who are passionate about the mission and vision of the organization. But that passion doesn't automatically translate into commitment to each task or project.

When people are truly committed, because what they are doing is aligned with their personal desires or needs, they will go above and beyond minimum expectations.

When have you been truly committed to achieving a goal? Were you committed because someone else asked you to be? Probably not.

You were committed because you saw the opportunity to make a difference, to solve a problem or to help another person who was important to you.

As a leader, remember to find out why others are committed to your organization or team. Don't assume they are committed for the same reasons you are. Find ways for others to demonstrate their commitment by being sure they are assigned some tasks or responsibilities that match their reasons for being involved.

Authority helps you manage. Commitment helps you lead.

Think . . . and act . . . like a leader!

"Discomfort from confrontation can provide great growth. If you're not experiencing any resistance, you're not moving forward."
A. S. Tolbert

Why do we think we're doing our best job when everything is going smoothly? Or maybe the real question should be, why do we think we're not handling our jobs well when people are asking questions or challenging the way things are done?

Leaders are needed to take organizations into new territory. Leaders are needed to solve problems. Leaders are needed to encourage and empower staff to improve productivity.

All those options require leaders to hear about what doesn't work and what needs to change.

So, if you can't handle confrontation in a positive way, you most likely won't be a great leader.

If you create an environment where peers or subordinates are afraid to bring you issues, you most likely won't be viewed as a great leader.

If you are not skilled at bringing problems out into the open and working with others to create better solutions, then you most likely aren't a great leader.

This month, invite others to "push back" on your ideas. Ask people who work with you on a regular basis to give you feedback about how you handle confrontation. Make a commitment to ask people to tell you the potential problems in your strategies.

It might be a little uncomfortable at first . . . but over time it will be easier.

Think . . . and act . . . like a leader!

"Time is neutral. It can be used either destructively or constructively."

Martin Luther King Jr.

Think of the biggest problems your organization faces. Now compare those problems to diseases or conditions we might face in the human body.

If your body has a sore throat you would treat that differently than you would treat a diagnosis of cancer. Likewise, in your organization, you need to respond to different problems with different healing strategies! It is important to consult with others and develop a structured treatment plan, just as you would do if your health was threatened by illness.

No matter what the "illness" is in your organization, your perspective as the leader will set the tone for how others recognize and respond to the challenge ahead.

I used to think healing seemed to take such a long time . . . until I realized that (except in cases of accidents or unexpected injuries)it takes our bodies an even longer time to get to the point where we are so sick we need medication, surgery or therapy. So now I try to adjust my thinking to appreciate how amazing it is that the body can heal itself in months from what took years to develop.

For example, the first time I was scheduled for acupuncture a part of me was hoping for an immediate cure in one or two visits. But the reality was that I had been having intense sciatica-like pain for almost a full year before I resorted to acupuncture.

After the 8th acupuncture treatment, when I realized my body was almost back to normal, I got excited. In less than 11 weeks this amazing human body (with a little help from acupuncture and other therapy) had practically reversed what had slowly escalated into a health crisis over 11 months.

So as you work to heal the dysfunctional behavior or management challenges in your organization, remember it will take time. If it took 4 years to create the problem you are not going to fix it in 4 weeks or by sending out a couple of emails.

If you are an effective leader, you will patiently and consistently carry out a treatment plan that heals the problem. And the time it takes you to fix the problems will be only a fraction of the time it took for each problem to develop and grow.

Think . . . and act . . . like a leader!

"If you always do what you always did, you will always get what you always got."
Jackie "Moms" Mabley

So often we find ourselves setting the same goal year after year because we haven't achieved it. We know it is a goal we want to achieve. We know it's a goal that is important to the organization. But we haven't been able to make much progress; so we simply set the same goal again.

When that happens . . . there's probably nothing wrong with the goal. More likely, the problem is with our choices about how to reach the goal.

The problem is in our behavior, not in our beliefs. What we think about, what we say and what we do to reach the goal is simply not getting the job done. Yet, at the beginning of the next year we set the same goal and tell ourselves we will surely achieve the goal if we "just keep trying."

Then another 12 months goes by and we have little progress despite our commitment and our passion.

I say, "Stop the delusion."

Starting today . . . stop thinking, saying and doing the same things you've been thinking, saying and doing for the past three years. If you honestly want to achieve the goal and if you really want a different result . . . you must think, say and do different things.

Think . . . and act . . . like a leader!

"If you don't like where you are in life, there comes a point when you must give up the part of you that's keeping you back."

Dr. Sonya Friedman

Complain, complain, complain!

When I get tired of hearing myself complain about the same problems or challenges I usually remember that I am the common denominator
in each of these situations.

So, I first consider if I can change the situation. I investigate whether or not I can easily resolve the challenge or get others to help me.

But, if I can't change the situation, and it's something I need to continue to deal with, I start looking at what I can change about myself.

Ask yourself, "What things am I doing that I know hold me back from the success I could be having?" Then commit to eliminating bad habits, learning new skills, building a stronger support network . . . or doing whatever you need to do.

Then ask yourself, "What beliefs or behaviors do I need to let go of if I really want to be a better leader?" Make a commitment to do what it takes to improve!

The journey to a better future begins with the choices you make today.

Think . . . and act . . . like a leader!

"Think of it as evolution instead of failure."
Kym I. King

My friend Kym King is a very wise woman. She had been struggling with achieving a goal that was very important to her. For several years she gave this goal serious attention. She planned. She sought out support. She studied. She tried different approaches. She made progress, but never felt she had accomplished the goal.

Has that ever happened to you? As a leader you may have projects that never seem to end, or people you always seem to have difficulty with. You feel as if you have failed because you haven't achieved your goal or because you are still working on developing the skill or nurturing the relationship.

Maybe you can do what Kym did.

One day she acknowledged she had achieved some success; some progress had been made. She took note of the things that had moved her closer to her goal.

That helped her realize she was evolving from one point of success to the next. And in time, those successes would lead her to achieving either the original goal or something much better.

As leaders we often set lofty goals and high standards. We must remember we can only achieve those goals by stringing many small successes together.

Don't forget that each success is progress toward the bigger goal . . . and the end result may not look like you imagined!

Think . . . and act . . . like a leader!

Everyone yearns for a better life. Yet few people take even the smallest steps in that direction."

Susan L. Taylor

To paraphrase Susan Taylor's words, "Everyone yearns for a better organization. Yet few people will do the work it takes to get the desired result."

Are you the complainer? The one who tells everyone why you can't complete the tasks you've agreed to do?

Or maybe you are the phantom leader. That's the leader who never seems to be around when there's trouble, but can always be found when successes are achieved.

You may be the broken record . . . repeating the same goals and the same action list week after week, month after month and maybe even year after year. Your list of action items stays the same because you're always talking about what you are going to do even though you never seem to complete any significant goals.

Or are you the critic? You can see exactly what every other person has done wrong or why new ideas won't work?

What our organizations need are more people who will take one small step after another toward positive change. It doesn't take much. You don't have to do it all in one big, dramatic effort.

Be the leader who not only wants a better organization but is also willing to do the work it takes to improve processes, encourage people and serve customers.

Think . . . and act . . . like a leader!

"Words can hurt and words can heal. What did your words do today?"
Rosie Horner

As human beings we often say (or write things in email) without thinking about how the person who receives those words might hear (or read) them.

This week, slow down long enough to read each email you write from the perspective of the recipient. Slow down enough to really think about the words you use in meetings and on the phone. Stay alert for any patterns that might be building walls, instead of bridges, between you and others.

Take a few minutes to CHOOSE your words and your tone. Be intentional. What you say and write will either build your team and your organization or tear them apart, one conversation at a time.

As leaders, we have a responsibility to be careful with our words.

Think . . . and act . . . like a leader!

"Instead of changing addresses, address the issue."
Eric Allenbough

During times of frustration it's human to feel like giving up. Sometimes we change jobs because we are simply tired of facing the same people or the same problems over and over.

If you walk away from a persistent performance issue with a subordinate, or if you leave policies in place that don't serve the organization, the person who follows you will have to clean up your mess.

Stop postponing that difficult conversation. Stop avoiding the research.

To help you get started, I suggest you write a clear description of what progress or success will look like. Then establish a 12 point plan to improve the situation. (A 12-point plan is a plan with one goal per month for 12 months, or one goal per week for 12 weeks.) Take some form of concrete action this week to begin your journey.

Think . . . and act . . . like a leader!

"Like a rubber ball, the harder you get thrown down signifies the higher you'll rise when you bounce back"

Langston Hughes

Feeling hopeless, afraid, embarrassed or stuck? Good!

Good? Why would I describe these emotions most people would label bad as good?

When you only experience success you develop a false sense of strength and it is easy to slip into the trap of perfectionism.

Let your difficulties teach you lessons about perseverance, teambuilding, planning, trust and the importance of life-long learning.

When faced with major problems, do you tend to GO through the pain, complaining and whining along the way? Do you feel sorry for yourself and seek sympathy from your friends and colleagues? Do you look for others to blame? Do you seek revenge or just wait for it to pass?

Next time, choose to GROW through the challenge, learning and sharing at each stage. Don't get stuck in the pain and fear.

Look for friends and colleagues who can help you understand the lessons in the difficulty.

Try to find at least one positive outcome that can come from the frustration you are feeling right now. Acknowledging where you are, but staying focused on where you are going, is a great strategy.

We all have setbacks. They make you feel like you are a glass window recently shattered by an unexpected brick being thrown through it.

What separates the consistent achievers from others is their ability to use their setbacks as bricks in their foundation for future success.

Think . . . and act . . . like a leader!

"You must genuinely like and respect those who are performing under your command, for neither the liking nor the respect can be successfully faked."
Benjamin Davis

"I don't go to work to make friends."

"I don't care if they like me or not; but they better respect me!"

Have you heard those two lines before? Have you SAID those two lines?

As a leader, it is important that you have both a friendly and a respectful relationship with the people in your department and with those who are working on your team.

Being friendly does not mean you participate in social events away from work. But it does mean that you connect with people on a personal level. You see them as individual people. You know what they care about. You recognize their unique skills, talents or experiences and appreciate the differences they bring.

As a leader, it is also critical that respect goes both ways. You expect to be respected because of your role or position. But people tend to respect you based on the way you demonstrate respect for them.

If you are working with people on a team or project or community board of directors who you don't like, make a special effort to find one or two things you have in common. Then focus on your shared values, your shared commitments or your shared passion for the work you are doing together. This will give you a reason to like and respect this person and your work together will be more productive.

Remember, as the leader, it is YOUR responsibility to make the team dynamics work. The example you set for connecting with each individual in an authentic and respectful way will set the tone for others.

Think . . . and act . . . like a leader!

"I used to want the words "She tried" on my tombstone. Now I want "She did it."
Katherine Dunham

"No excuse is acceptable." With this simple line a mentor in my past changed my life.

He had drilled this message into his sons for years. He taught them that making excuses was at best, wasted breath, and at worse, a crack in the foundation of integrity. And when I was in my 20s he taught me this principle by his example as a leader in the church and in the community where he lived.

This idea -- that making excuses for failure to perform simply was not an option -- really resonated with me. But it wasn't because I thought I could be perfect at everything I tried.

When things don't work out the way I thought they would, I would rather admit to a failure with Plan A and then get busy developing and executing Plan B.

I would rather ask for help and involve others to achieve a large goal than let it fail because I felt I had to do it alone. I would rather decline an invitation or request that I knew I could not fulfill than tell someone I would do something I had no intention of doing.

These choices all related to my belief that you do not blame others when something does not work out the way you planned. Instead, as a leader, you are responsible for figuring out what needs to be done-- and who needs to be involved -- to achieve the goals. (And every now and then you might have to change the goals!)

My mentor taught me, through his words and his daily example, that excuses were not productive. You accomplish your goal or you don't. You fulfill your promises or you don't. And to avoid excuses the most important thing is to be very careful about what you commit to in the first place!

He also taught me that when I hear an excuse forming in my mind, ask myself if there is something that is more important to express than the excuse. Apologies for disappointing others are more effective. Learning lessons from the failures is more critical. Strategies for moving forward are more powerful.

When we are honest with ourselves about what we can, and can not do, it is easy to lead others toward a mutually agreed upon goal.

Think . . . and act . . . like a leader!

"The most dangerous leadership myth is that leaders are born—that there is a genetic factor to leadership. This myth asserts that people simply either have certain charismatic qualities or not. That's nonsense; in fact, the opposite is true. Leaders are made rather than born."

Warren Bennis

Here is how he describes the difference between a manager and a leader:

- Managers administer, leaders innovate
- Managers ask how and when, leaders ask what and why
- Managers focus on systems, leaders focus on people
- Managers do things right, leaders do the right things
- Managers maintain, leaders develop
- Managers rely on control, leaders inspire trust
- Managers have a short-term perspective, leaders have a longer-term perspective
- Managers accept the status-quo, leaders challenge the status-quo
- Managers have an eye on the bottom line, leaders have an eye on the horizon

- Managers imitate, leaders originate
- Managers emulate the classic good soldier, leaders are their own person
- Managers copy, leaders show originality

Think . . . and act . . . like a leader!

"An organization with an indispensable man is guilty of management failure."

H.S. Hook

Don't let one person hold all the information about a project, a department, an organization or an event. This person will start to think of him or herself as indispensable. Even worse others on the team may also start to think nothing can happen without input or leadership from this individual.

When someone is indispensable in that way it definitely points to mismanagement and lack of leadership.

I once worked with a man who purposely withheld information. John would treat people badly and behave inappropriately but the organization wouldn't fire him because no one else was prepared to step into his projects or responsibilities.

However, all employees who seem indispensable aren't problem employees. Another person I worked with was regarded as indispensable because she was a self-starter. Mary would constantly look for opportunities to solve problems or to work on projects no one else wanted to be involved in.

Unfortunately, one weekend she was killed in a car accident and the organization was not prepared to maintain the programs and projects she had been working on. They experienced major delays, incurred quite a bit of expense and lost both productivity and revenue while others tried to 'get up to speed' on Mary's projects.

This week look around your team or organization. Who is indispensible? Establish a structured plan to insure there are others ready to step in to support or replace that 'indispensable' person.

Think . . . and act . . . like a leader!

"Who is Robert - and why do we still follow his rules anyway?"

Alice Collier Cochran

I've been reading a really wonderful book titled, "Roberta's Rules of Order: A Guide for Nonprofits and Other Teams." One day the author, Alice Cochran, was facilitating a tense meeting with a dysfunctional community group. A member of the group was quite insistent that Robert's Rules of Order be used. Others in the group were not in support of that. Ms. Cochran suggested they use "Roberta's" rules instead.

Of course, Roberta's Rules of Order did not exist until that moment.

But while working with that group, and with many other groups during subsequent years, the author developed a set of processes and problem-solving strategies she has found to be very successful for boards and other teams.

Sometimes, as leaders, it is crucial for us to change the process.

Always, as leaders, it's important for us to choose the correct process for each situation or team we are leading.

So don't get stuck in the way you have always done things. And don't force the process you are most comfortable with on everyone else just because it is a process or strategy you are comfortable with.

Don't go for complex and bureaucratic when simple and participative will be more effective. Don't structure conversations as debate when dialogue is needed. Don't ask for consensus when an executive decision needs to be made. Get the picture?

It's your job to know more than one process and to use what is most appropriate to get results with the current team. Even better, learn ways to guide the team in the development of its own customized processes and systems!

In other words, the best leaders pay attention to the group or team they are leading and adapt to that group's needs and style.

Think . . . and act . . . like a leader!

"Being given a particular organizational title may confer some hierarchical authority, but it certainly does not make you a leader."
Rob Goffee & Gereth Jones

Have you ever been frustrated because people who reported to you just didn't do what you told them to do?

Have you ever avoided going to a meeting where you were the chairperson or the 'leader' of the group because half the group members were out of control or following their own direction instead of yours?

Both situations are warning signs that you might be a good manager but you are not being a good leader.

And if you have never found yourself in either of these situations you are either an amazing leader or you are a terrible leader who is in denial!

Most of us became leaders because we had strong technical skills or because we had strong project management skills. The natural progression was to have us manage people in order to oversee more projects or to help others learn our technical skills.

But if you are like me you've learned over time that the same skills you use to manage projects are not always directly applicable to managing and leading people.

So if you've been relying on your title as a demand for respect and trust, reconsider your approach. Leadership is all about creating a shared vision, helping others be successful and building strong relationships while you move toward a goal.

Authority is important. But the best leaders know that in order to get long-lasting results and maximum productivity, authenticity beats authority every time.

Think . . . and act . . . like a leader!

"Good leaders make others good leaders."
Michael Brundy

A most important measure of your success as a leader is the number of good leaders you develop, groom and mentor.

Can you look back at previous leadership roles and identify one or more people who went from working for you to being fabulously respected leaders in future roles? Have you had people who reported to you come back a few years later and tell you specific things you did that helped shape their leadership style?

This week, commit to helping at least one person on your team become a better leader.

Remember that leadership is not only about what you do now to accomplish today's goals. It is also about what you do now to develop strong leaders who can step into critical leadership roles in the future.

Think . . . and act . . . like a leader!

"Every company has two organizational structures: the formal one is written on the charts; the other is the living relationship of the men and women in the organization."

H. Green

I bet you have heard of 'the good ol' boy's network'. The idea that men share information with each other to insure the success of their friends is nothing new. It is just one example of an informal system for getting things done.

The org chart for our organization does tell us who is accountable for certain functions. But the org chart tells us nothing about the informal way people actually accomplish their responsibilities.

It is important to know the informal network of leaders and the informal communication channels people in your organization use to make decisions, to make suggestions and to share information. Successful leaders use both the formal structure and the informal system to achieve the desired goals.

Think . . . and act . . . like a leader!

"Come out from behind yourself into the conversation and make it real."

Susan Scott

I might adapt Susan Scott's quote to say: "Come out from behind your WORDS into the conversation and make it real."

Many managers find themselves caught in the trap of using words as a shield to protect themselves from being questioned or challenged.

Too often we find managers using words to impress others with their intelligence or to defend their worthiness to be in a position of power.

And sometimes we find ourselves using words to manipulate outcome in situations where collaboration is the expressed goal.

As leaders we must use words to communicate complex ideas, important strategies and critical priorities.

We also must use words to convey our feelings, to let people know we care about them and the business priorities and to resolve sensitive issues.

But all too often our words conceal simple truth, confuse the people we are talking with and create bigger barriers to building trust.

Of course we need words. But exceptional leaders tend to use the simplest words possible in order to reach more people more quickly.

Leaders who are outstanding communicators ask directly for what they want or need from others.

And excellent leaders use words to reveal how their personal values and beliefs integrate with the priorities they are driving in the group or organization.

This week, say more with fewer words. Come out from behind your words and let the people you engage with connect to your commitment, your concern and your compassion. Think about how you use words in important conversations.

Think . . . and act . . . like a leader!

"Why are you so afraid to say what is true for you? Do you think I can not handle your truth? Or do you think I can not handle the ways we differ?"
Tracy Brown

Last week I was speaking at a conference for nonprofit leaders. My subject was about building (and rebuilding) trust within the Board of Directors.

One woman shared that her organization's Board meetings were always pleasant. People were cooperative. There was never any conflict.

I said, "Most likely there is very little trust between your Board members and you are probably a victim of The Conspiracy of Courtesy(tm)."

She looked at me for a long couple of seconds and then thoughtfully said, "You're probably right."

As a leader, one of your jobs is to create an environment where people can share their ideas and concerns. If no one ever takes that risk they have gotten the message that it is not acceptable to have a controversial view. Or, maybe they have picked up on a culture where you are only rewarded for being pleasant and making others comfortable with you.

Great leaders don't create controversy for controversy's sake; but instead encourage and support differing opinions on critical subjects.

Great leaders take risks and encourage others on their teams to take risks with each other.

Great leaders know that everyone won't agree and everyone won't like each other all the time.

Think . . . and act . . . like a leader!

> **"The ultimate measure of a man is not where he stands in moments of comfort and convenience, but where he stands in times of challenge and controversy."**
> **Martin Luther King, Jr.**

It is so easy to be a leader when there is money in the bank, your organization has a good reputation and all the press you are getting is good press.

But do you have what it takes to be a leader when the organization has faced 6 consecutive quarters of losses, your industry is in decline or an investigative reporter has uncovered a weak link in your products or services?

Often the line is drawn in the sand between a good manager and a good leader as a result of negative results or unexpected complaints. Great leaders excel when tensions are high and there is no path to success to follow.

Are you able to inspire and lead people in your organization through tough times? How good are you at being tough but also engaging people with different ideas to find a solution to a new problem?

Do people bring you the tough issues and the terrible news with fear and trepidation? Or do they come to you knowing and trusting that you will find a way to succeed in spite of the challenge they are asking you to take on?

This week I dare you to ask people who know you well if you are a leader in times of controversy and change!

Think . . . and act . . . like a leader!

"I have a great belief in the fact that whenever there is chaos, it creates wonderful thinking. I consider chaos a gift."

Septima P Clark

All too often we think our job as a leader is to avoid chaos.

Or if chaos exists we think we are supposed to solve the problem and get things running smoothly again as quickly as possible.

But what would happen if we instead embraced chaos as "a gift?" How would that change our response?

Isn't it true that chaos is always the precursor of change? Things have to get a little messy before we recognize the need to improve systems or processes.

And it seems to me that lots of creative ideas come out of the minds and hearts of people who need to find a new solution or learn a new skill (because the world as they knew it has changed).

Good leaders expect chaos and are ready to face it head on. Great leaders are inspired by chaos and prepare to capture the greatness from the situation with calm and focused guidance.

Think . . . and act . . . like a leader!

"Fear is the single greatest obstacle to success"
Dennis Kimbro

- What are you afraid to try?
- What are you afraid to finish?
- What are you afraid to talk about?
- Who are you afraid to challenge?
- Who are you afraid will challenge you?
- What role is fear playing in your success?
- Do you realize that everyone has fears -- including the greatest of leaders?

Fears are a natural part of life. It means you are on the edge of new territory. Fear is a natural response to the unknown. Fear is a human emotion designed to warn you to be careful.

But fear is NOT designed to paralyze you!

This week, think about the fears that are holding you back from being a great leader. Consider why you are afraid. Then take one action step beyond your fears and toward your goals.

Think . . . and act . . . like a leader!

"When you find a man who has lost his way, you don't make fun of him and scorn him and leave him there. You show him the way. If you don't do that you just prove that you're sort of lost yourself."
Zora Neale Hurston

Step off your pedestal of superiority.

Share the information you have that might help others succeed. Mentor someone who is traveling a path you have already travelled. Coach someone who has great potential but needs a little help to get to their next level of success. Give constructive feedback to someone who is headed in the wrong direction but doesn't know it.

Focus on being of service to others and your success will be supported by those you have helped.

Think . . . and act . . . like a leader!

"It is only those who are free inside who can help those around them."

Peter Abrahams

Independence Day. On the Fourth of July we celebrate the independence of the United States of America. It is a federal holiday celebrating the adoption of the Declaration of Independence on July 4, 1776, declaring independence from the Kingdom of Great Britain.

Emancipation Day. The Emancipation Proclamation was signed by President Abraham Lincoln on January 1, 1863. Slavery was outlawed and all slaves in the United States were declared free.

Are people in your organization wishing for an Independence Day? Are they hoping and praying for freedom from tyrannical rule or inhumane oppression?

I hope it's not that bad. But this is a great time to think about what makes people free? What is freedom really about? And what elements of freedom or independence are critical to building a productive culture in your organization?

Our country's founding fathers signed the Declaration of

Independence. It is a fine document that describes the vision for our freedom. It states the ideals upon which we have created a nation.

Abraham Lincoln wrote and signed the Emancipation Proclamation. It clearly described who would be emancipated and within what time frame.

But signing a document that declares freedom or independence isn't enough. Freedom is an inner state of being; a way of thinking and acting.

So, as a leader, you must do more than set a policy of freedom, respect, independence and cooperation. You must create the mindset and the environment that encourages people to be free, but also to cooperate within the general rules and guidelines that have been established.

And because freedom begins with an inner sense of self-respect, what are you doing to insure that people in your organization know their talents, skills and unique point of view is valued by you and your organization?

This week consider what employees in your organization need in order to feel free to consistently contribute their best to achieve the goals of your organization.

Think . . . and act . . . like a leader!

"Everybody has barriers and obstacles. If you look at them as containing fences that don't allow you to advance, then you're going to be a failure. If you look at them as hurdles that strengthen you each time you go over one, then you're going to be a success."

Dr. Benjamin Carson

It is so easy to look at the people you think of as good leaders and say, "Wow, they just have natural talent as a leader." Or, "She's such a great leader; look how smoothly her operation runs."

Let me assure you . . . that leader faces many barriers and obstacles you just don't know about.

Great leaders know that obstacles and barriers are part of the job. If there were no barriers or obstacles to getting the job done there would not be a need for a leader!

So this week, acknowledge your barriers as stepping stones to success and take them in your stride. Don't fight them; welcome them. Don't ignore them; deal with them. Don't deny them; attack them with a plan of action designed to eliminate them!

Think . . . and act . . . like a leader!

"I have no mercy or compassion in me for a society that will crush people and then penalize them for not being able to stand up under the weight."
Malcolm X

Ok, stay with me here.

Malcolm X was talking about the politics and oppression in the United States of America. But when I think about many of the corporations I am familiar with, I hear employees talking about the politics and the unfair circumstances they experience.

And it's not just the big mega-corporations. I see this happening in associations (non-profit corporations), government agencies (federal corporations), church organizations (religious corporations) and small businesses (partnerships or micro-corporations).

Too often people are left to "sink or swim" or to find their own way in a complex organization. It becomes a rite of passage if you can survive your first six months in a new assignment since you weren't given the tools, information or resources you needed to succeed with ease.

As a leader, have you ever thought about the way working or serving in your organization might feel to the average person?

Does your organization "crush" people? Ignore their ideas? Challenge their self-esteem? Deny them opportunities to develop their skills and talents?

And then, after crushing them do they get penalized for not being superstars for not thinking outside of the box? For not taking the initiatives to serve clients more effectively?

Your organization is a society. And you, the leader, have the ability (and responsibility) to create a culture that either nourishes or destroys the human spirit. What is your choice?

Think . . . and act . . . like a leader!

"XPS M2010: Ultimate Innovation."
Dell

Dell has a new computer. It's not a desk top. It's not a lap top. It's both. (With a 20" super-thin monitor, a removable wireless keyboard, a video cam built in and lots of other features I didn't know I needed until now.)

The model number is XPS-M2010 & I don't know where they came up with that model name. But I'm guessing that during the design process someone said, "What do we think our customers will want in the year 2010?" Then they proceeded to design this amazing machine that is unlike anything else on the market.

And we, the consumer, can buy this computer now . . . four years before we even realized it has everything we could possibly want in the future!

Now, I'm not writing about this just to tell you about this new computer. (Even though I seriously do want one.) I'm also thinking about us as leaders.

What would happen if you asked yourself as a leader, "What will people need from me 4 years from now?" then got serious about preparing yourself to meet those needs?

What would you have to do differently for people in your organization to be standing in line to work with you because you are the leader they consider to be at the forefront of excellence and integrity?

What would have to change in your performance for people who work with you to say, "Wow! There isn't anyone else like her! She is the best leader we have."

If Dell can design and sell a computer that represents "ultimate innovation" why can't we redesign and reinvent our leadership skills?

This week, consider how you might repackage yourself to become tomorrow's best leader.

Think . . . and act . . . like a leader!

"An adventure is only an inconvenience, rightly considered."

G. K. Chesterton

What little inconvenience irritated you last week?

What recurring inconvenience frustrated you during the past month?

How many things do we let get under our skin because they are inconveniences that take us slightly off course and make us adapt or change our planned activities?

As leaders, it is our job to guide the project or the team toward success. We know things won't always go exactly as planned.

So next time an inconvenience welcomes itself into my world I am going to "flip the script." I am going to remind myself to think about the inconvenience as today's opportunity to take a little adventure on the leadership journey.

I'm going to think of these unexpected inconveniences with the same perspective I use when I think of my vacation: "How can I make this fun, educational or inspiring?"

This week, I invite you to view your inconveniences through the lens of adventure.

Think . . . and act . . . like a leader!

"When we turn our backs on feelings we should deal with, they fester and grow and ultimately consume us. Silence is denial. Silence is anxiety."

Susan Taylor

"Emotions have no place in the workplace." Have you ever heard that?

I heard that line dozens of times in the early years of my career.

But it never made sense to me that you could expect people to do their best work if they weren't allowed to express emotion.

And it never made sense to me that managers would not want to know about things they were doing that made workers feel uncomfortable or disrespected or ignored.

As a leader you don't need to know or understand every emotion every person feels or experiences. But I encourage you to create opportunities to hear about employees' feelings - especially their feelings related to the work you are doing and the way the team interacts with one another.

Find ways to make it safe for people to share the highs and the lows that influence their productivity. Don't wait until emotions are so bottled up they spill out uncontrollably as a result of stress, fear, anger or hopelessness.

Great leaders understand that emotional silence is denial of humanity . . . and denial of humanity results in robot-like performance.

This week, break the silence.

Think . . . and act . . . like a leader!

"If you understood everything I say, you'd be me."
Miles Davis

Next time someone on your team doesn't quite understand what you are saying remember this quote!

So often we forget that the people we interact with might know us very well but they will never become us. So it is inevitable that there will be those times when miscommunication results in misunderstanding.

You might be pretty wonderful, with great talents and valuable experience. But I hope you would agree with me that you don't want every person to be just like you, think just like you and do everything the exact way you would do it.

One of the best benefits of leading a team is having an opportunity to experience ways different approaches and different stylescan achieve success.

Remember, your job as the leader is to provide clear vision, general guidelines and the resources people need to achieve the group goals.

Don't get sidetracked by expecting everyone to act or think just like you.

And definitely don't get mad when someone doesn't understand everything you say the first time you say it!

Great leaders have the ability to communicate their message, and the organization's needs, in different ways in order to connect with different stakeholders.

This week, polish your communication skills.

Think . . . and act . . . like a leader!

"Lots of times you have to pretend to join a parade in which you're not really interested in order to get where you're going."

George Morley

True confession. When I started writing this weekly e-zine on leadership I wasn't really interested in becoming a better leader.

I was primarily motivated by a desire to challenge others to step up THEIR leadership skills so we could together improve a national association we were all involved in.

So I kinda joined a parade called "let's celebrate leadership and make a big deal out it."

I started making leadership the "party line" and talked about it all the time as one of the core elements necessary for our growth and future success. I invited people to subscribe to this e-zine. I started giving people recommendations about specific books on the topic of leadership that I had found helpful.

In the beginning, this was just a tool to use to get me where I was really going. I hitched a ride on one of the parade cars and started waving at the crowd hoping to inspire them and encourage them to become better leaders. But my real destination was association growth and stability. The leadership parade was just a part of getting to the other side of town.

However, it didn't take long for me to realize just how much I needed this series of weekly reminders too! The discipline of writing them forced me to follow through on commitments. The process of writing them helped me further clarify the elements of leadership I believed in the most. The challenge of writing them drove me to search for quotations from varied sources I might not have otherwise picked up. The responsibility of writing them helped me regularly return to my dreams for the association and my hopes for our progress.

I definitely have become a better leader as a result of choosing to help others improve their leadership knowledge and skills.

So I may have started off "pretending" to be a member of the leadership band in a parade celebrating excellence; but now I'm the drum major and loving it! The word has spread well beyond our association. Clients and audience members have subscribed then spread the word to their coworkers and friends.

So what parade are you in that is just a way to get you to a bigger goal? Are there things you are doing because it is expected of you or because it's just the right thing to do? This week, instead of just going through the motions, stop and reflect on the unexpected benefits you have derived from marching on that particular parade route. Then celebrate the gifts that parade has brought into your life.

Think . . . and act . . . like a leader!

"Fear is the energy to do your best in a new situation. The feeling of fear is really preparation energy. It's getting you ready to excel, to succeed, to do your best and to learn the most."

John-Rogers & Peter McWilliams

I love this quote! Thinking of fear as PREPARATION energy is so healthy!

But most of us think of fear as PARALYSIS energy. We notice our fear and we back away from taking the next step. We recognize our fear and we freeze up. We hide our fear by doing more of what we already know instead of taking on new challenges and meeting new people.

This week, look at your fears and say, "Isn't this great that I'm so afraid? Here are three things I am going to do so I can get through the fear and get to my next success!"

Think . . . and act . . . like a leader!

"Losers visualize the penalties of failure. Winners visualize the rewards of success."
Rob Gilbert

I really wanted that contract to deliver a keynote speech to the managers and supervisors of a large city government staff. I thought it would be exciting to inspire them to focus on customer service.

I could imagine them saying, "Wow!" as I shared examples of what local citizens had told me about their expectations. I smiled when I envisioned the standing ovation and the line of people wanting to talk to me after the speech.

So, when I went in for a preliminary meeting with the selection team I was passionate, convincing and definitely on my "A" game.

It worked. I made the first cut! Winners visualize the rewards of success.

During that meeting I had asked the committee about the selection and approval process. They shared a pretty typical series of steps that included approvals by the City Manager and presentation to the City Council. Not a big deal, right?

Wrong. I continued to think about the audience and the speech at least once a day. But I couldn't stop thinking almost every hour about all the things that could go wrong between the committee liking me and the city council approving the expenditure.

I started envisioning a city manager who didn't want me because he had a colleague he had virtually promised the job to.

I had a dream that the city council saw my company name on the consent agenda and three people asked questions that resulted in the approval process being delayed.

I started practicing how I would respond to a long list of objections I was sure the committee was going to offer.

I even began calculating how much I could reduce the fee the committee had already approved because this was, after all, a not for profit government entity and I didn't want to lose the visibility because I was charging too much.

I kept saying to myself that I was going to be selected and I was going to do a fabulous job . . . but every time I visualized the event in my mind now, the audience was looking back at me with blank stares and a guy in the first row was sleeping. My confidence was shaken.

So it's no surprise that I was actually relieved when I got the voice message saying they had narrowed it down to me and one other speaker but had selected the other speaker.

Losers visualize the penalties of failure.

What you visualize makes a huge difference in your ability to lead yourself, and others, toward achieving your goals.

Leaders are winners. Attach your energy to visualizing the rewards of success and watch your success grow.

Think . . . and act . . . like a leader!

"The best way to escape from a problem is to solve it."

Brendan Francis

What's the problem that never seems to go away? It's driving you crazy. You just want it to disappear. You want to escape!

Well you can. You can escape the stress, the fear and the frustration of this problem by simply solving it.

First, understand the problem and its root causes. Block out everything else for 15 minutes and jot down what you know about the problem and why it occurs or recurs.

Next, make two lists. On one list write down what you can influence. On the other list write the actions or people you have no control over.

Third, brainstorm all the things you might do that would reduce or eliminate the problem.

Finally, pick three things (no more) that you will do to help you or your team move toward a solution.

That final step of taking three concrete actions will work wonders for you as a leader. And after you see results from those firs three steps, select your three next steps. Chip away at the problem until it is no longer causing you frustration.

Once you have done everything you can do; even if there are still some problems you will not feel frustrated, helpless or victimized. You will know you have done all you can do and it will be easier to assign accountability for the problem where it rightfully belongs.

Problems don't just disappear. They don't evaporate into thin air because you wish them to be gone. But escaping problems is as easy as solving them.

Think . . . and act . . . like a leader!

"If you don't have confidence, you'll always find a way not to win."
Carl Lewis

Be sure, as a leader, that you have confidence in the direction you are leading the team. There may not be anything worse than the leader who is telling the troops to go in one direction while he quietly goes in a different direction.

If you don't have confidence in the strategy and tactics being deployed, how can others?

If you believe you will fail you will.

Think . . . and act . . . like a leader!

"He not busy being born is busy dying."
Bob Dylan

Unlike some of you I am not really a Bob Dylan fan. But I do love this quote.

It reminds me that being born is all about looking at the world with a fresh set of eyes. Being born is about being a leader who is alert to trends and opportunities with a focus on the future.

Don't get so stuck in your ways you are closer to death than life. Be careful about focusing on doing things the way they have always been done in the past; especially when the challenges you face could never have existed ten (or even five) years ago!

Good leaders develop new skills, ask probing questions and encourage people around them to grow.

Great leaders work from a solid set of values but evolve in the ways they apply those values to new situations and people.

Think . . . and act . . . like a leader!

"The inferior teacher tells you that something is wrong with you and offers to fix it. The superior teacher tells you that something is right with you and helps you bring it forth."
Alan Cohen

When you stepped into your current leadership role what kind of advice did you receive from your predecessor. And what kind of information did you receive from the people you would be working most closely with?

Were you told all about the problems that exist, or the opportunities ahead?

Were the faults of each of your direct reports or colleagues described, or did you instead hear more about their strengths?

Were you given the list of past failures and organizational potholes to avoid, or were you encouraged to know about, and build upon, the recent successes of the organization?

I ask you these questions because the answers will give you a snapshot of whether you are a part of an organization where the culture is grounded in what is going well or what is going poorly.

But remember: regardless of the organization's culture, you have a choice as a leader.

This week, look for that which is "right" in the people you lead. Help each person bring those skills, experiences, qualities and dreams into reality.

Identify the problems and weaknesses of the people you lead and evaluate how you can avoid assigning people roles or responsibilities for which they are not well suited.

Great leaders face the problems and weaknesses of the organization directly, efficiently and without a lot of fanfare. They give more exposure to what is going right and who is doing the right things.

Think . . . and act . . . like a leader!

"Let your life speak."
Quaker Principle

When you were growing up you probably heard adults say, "Actions speak louder than words."

Somewhere along the line you also picked up on the golden rule, "Do unto others as you would have them do unto you."

In the last decade, Stephen Covey reminded us "You can't talk yourself out of what you behave yourself into."

And there is a saying in the African American community that goes something like this: You're acting so loud I can't hear what you're saying!

Think about it.

People judge you based on what you do. They do not know what you are thinking. They do not know your genuine feelings. They can hear your words but don't know whether or not to believe them.

The only reliable source for judging what you know, what you feel and what you believe is to observe and experience your behavior.

The only way to demonstrate the commitment you have to specific values, priorities or goals is to demonstrate that commitment through visible and consistent behavior.

What is YOUR behavior telling people?

Think . . . and act . . . like a leader!

"Are you a leader because you want to receive the recognition, admiration and respect of others? Or are you a leader because the respect, admiration and respect of others has placed you in a position to lead?"

Tracy Brown

What would you be willing to do if no one could ever know you did it? Is your motivation improving the organization or improving your image?

Great leaders usually do both . . . but I'm asking you what is your primary motivation for stepping into the role of leader? It makes a huge difference.

Some of the worst leaders I have worked with through the years were in leadership roles primarily to be in power, to be in control and to have a certain title or position behind their name. They often didn't seem to care about (or didn't understand) the root problems and challenges people were facing; and they didn't develop the relationships required to provide long-term solutions.

They always took credit for the positive outcomes and almost always found someone else to blame when there were problems or negative results.

Some of the best leaders I have worked with through the years were actually introverts. They did not seek the limelight but understood they needed to be visible to achieve their goals for the organization. These leaders often let others share the spotlight when things were going well but always put themselves in the spotlight when tough decisions or difficult situations were being faced.

You don't need to be an introvert to be a great leader. But you do need to stay more focused on the organization's needs than your personal need for recognition and adoration.

If I were to interview people who reported to you, or your peers, which type of leader would they tell me you are?

Think . . . and act . . . like a leader!

"Courage is the atom of change."
Bettina Flores

Most of the time we are not looking for change but that doesn't keep it from happening! So the best leaders recognize when it is time to change and find a way to motivate themselves (and the people they are leading) to accept and adapt to the required change.

I agree with Ms Flores that leading in times of change requires great courage. Then again, almost all times are times of change. There always seems to be SOMETHING that requires a different approach, a new response or a fresh start.

It is courage that allows you to express a new vision unlike the one others currently see. It is courage that provides the fuel when the engine of your organization is about to run out of gas. It is courage that tells your reflection in the mirror to keep going when no one else can see the same vision you see.

One caution: don't confuse ego with courage. If you are the only one who sees a certain vision or feels the need to change and the predicted outcome is focused on your personal success or individual image then know you are not being driven by courage.

Leadership courage requires listening to the whisper that speaks an unconventional direction or choice that benefits the greater good.

Courage is the inner strength that nudges you forward to make a positive difference in the life and history of the organization when it would be easier to coast with the status quo.

Be courageous!

Think . . . and act . . . like a leader!

"The weirdest thing most of us do is avoid the very people we need to be around."
Sarano Kelley

When choosing the people we interact with, most of us will choose:

- Comfort over challenge
- Enjoyment over education
- Validation over exploring new values
- Agreement over accountability
- Compatibility over coaching

As leaders we need to include people in our inner circle who don't necessarily make our lives easier. Include people who share your vision but have different experiences, different education and different perspectives. They will challenge you but they will also expand your sphere of influence.

Think of a cousin, a parent, a spouse or a childhood friend who you trust. Do they always agree with you? Probably not. But you recognize they care about you and will give you "their view" of what you should do to achieve your goals.

How many times has someone like this given you a new idea, a fresh perspective, or advice you didn't like but later found it was the best advice you could have received?

So, as a leader, is there a way for you to create trusting and respectful relationships with people you don't always agree with?

These people will sometimes be difficult for you to like, but they will help you be a more effective (and more responsive) leader.

Identify at least one person who you know could provide deeper insight, great ideas or a different perspective. This needs to be someone you tend to avoid because it is uncomfortable for you to interact with him or her. This week, initiate a conversation with this person and expand your leadership perspective.

Think . . . and act . . . like a leader!

"Don't let yesterday use up too much of today."
Cherokee Proverb

Okay, so you blew it in yesterday's meeting. How long are you going to replay the error you made or the insensitive comment you made?

Apologize, fix the problem and focus on preparing for the next meeting.

Maybe you did something worse that that. Perhaps you lead a team that resulted in the organization losing thousands (or even millions) of dollars. Maybe you were laid off and now are afraid of losing your current job so you don't take any risks. Maybe your challenge didn't happen at work but as a result of things that occurred in your personal life you are stuck in a rut that is not serving your best interests.

You can not change the past. It is in the history books. It isn't going to get better (or worse) as a result of you thinking about it, talking about, or wishing you could change it.

So don't let yesterday take up too much of your time or your energy today!

As a leader, you also need to consider how much of yesterday's success you are using to validate your actions today. It is important to know, and respect, the organization's past. But it is critical to place your focus on the future and move toward that vision.

This week, notice how much time you spend rehashing the past. Then refocus your attention on your vision and the actions you need to take today to achieve your goals tomorrow.

Think . . . and act . . . like a leader!

"Everything will change. The only question is growing up or decaying."
Nikki Giovanni

Every morning is a fresh start. What happened yesterday is over. What will happen tomorrow is anybody's guess. But I guarantee that a year from now your life will not be exactly the same as it is now. There is always change.

As a leader, we sometimes fall into the trap of trying to keep everything "just like it is right now." Usually this is when things seem to be going well. People are getting along. We are making a profit (or at least breaking even). There just aren't a lot of problems to deal with.

We get in the "sweet spot" and forget that our job, as leaders, requires us to always keep the momentum moving in a positive direction. No change means stagnation - which leads to loss – which leads to death.

Stop equating change to crisis. Don't think change is only required when there are problems.

Remember the CQI (Continuous Quality Improvement) movement of the past? That was all about driving change to upgrade quality again and again and again. Getting better is a great change.

Become the leader who is known for continuous improvement.

Think . . . and act . . . like a leader!

"He who chatters with you will chatter of you."
Egyptian Proverb

Think about the last time you found yourself gossiping with someone about a coworker, colleague or friend.

Some of you only have to think back to yesterday, or a few minutes ago. But was it really necessary?

When we talk about the shortcomings or embarrassing moments of others we invite the people we talk to to do the same about us.

Wouldn't it be more productive to take complaints or observations directly to the person affected by them? As leaders, wouldn't we generate more respect if we held ourselves to a higher standard?

This week, join me in choosing to say only good things about people we work with. If we have a complaint, or a criticism, let's take it directly to the person.

Let us commit to making our "chatter" positive, affirming and respectful.

Think . . . and act . . . like a leader!

"The greatest threat to freedom is the absence of criticism."

Wole Soyinka

Last week I suggested you limit your chatter to comments that were positive, affirming and respectful. That doesn't mean we stop giving people feedback about what they can improve, change or learn.

The Soyinka quote refers to freedom but I invite you to replace that word with the word success:

"The greatest threat to success is the absence of criticism."

Think about it. Some of your greatest growth has come from feedback you received after screwing up, or from a mentor teaching you a better way to do something.

If you don't already know how to give constructive criticism learn as quickly as you can. Being able to give others feedback that helps them (and the organization) grow is a basic skill of an excellent leader.

Think . . . and act . . . like a leader!

"There is no such thing as a 'natural'. A natural dancer has to practice hard. A natural painter has to paint all the time. And a natural fool has to work at it."

Joe Louis

The greatest leaders I have personally met seemed to me to be "natural born leaders."

And there have been times I used that phrase to describe young people I have met or observed.

But the reality is that these leaders make it look natural because they recognize their talents - and the talents of others - and are consistent in moving themselves (and the organization) toward a goal.

Natural skills and talents may provide the foundation. But commitment and action provide the result.

If you have a talent for leadership that's great, but it doesn't mean you will automatically become, or be viewed by others as, a leader.

This week, evaluate what is innate, or natural, about your leadership success. Be thankful for it. Use it. And also be aware of that part of your leadership success that is the result of choice and hard work. Be grateful for that too. Continue it.

Think . . . and act . . . like a leader!

"Character, not circumstances, makes the man."

Booker T Washington

- What would you do if no one was watching?
- Would your hiring practices change if you weren't afraid of a discrimination lawsuit?
- Why do we need "insider trading" regulations?
- And what about Sarbanes-Oxley and all the policies that have been written since it was enacted?
- How will you handle the sick employee or board member who needs ongoing treatment for cancer?
- Would you make the same decisions if the employee or board member needed ongoing treatment for AIDS?
- What would you do if a friend admitted he beat his wife?
- How would you handle it if your neighbor committed suicide?
- If your assistant borrowed $10,000 from the company account what would you do?
- What if the money was to pay for medical care for his son?

We all know that character counts. Character is important. All these things might test your character. But character is not circumstantial.

Character is a constant that helps us choose the honorable path in difficult circumstances. Character is our guiding light in times of trouble. Character helps us keep our head up in times of stress or distress.

Great leaders are grounded and guided by character.

Think . . . and act . . . like a leader!

"Self-discipline, as a virtue or as an acquired asset, can be valuable to anyone."
Duke Ellington

How many times were you told, "Do the right thing" when you were growing up?

How many times have you told others, "You know that needs to be done; you don't need me to tell you or remind you every time."

Self-discipline is something we value. Self-discipline means doing what needs to be done without anyone else pushing us, reminding us or forcing us.

Great leaders have this inner discipline. It goes with responsibility, role modeling and getting results.

This week, notice all the ways you practice self-discipline; and acknowledge the people you work with who take initiative and do what needs to be done.

Think . . . and act . . . like a leader!

Some Closing Thoughts

Leadership is challenging. But it can also be very rewarding.

If you are like me, you need reminders on a regular basis to step up to the leadership challenge. Sometimes it would be so much easier to pout or procrastinate. Some days you just don't want to be bothered with putting others first. And all of us have months where we are so busy we just feel overwhelmed.

My goal is to remind you that leadership is the result of your daily, weekly and monthly choices. My goal is to encourage you to make being the best leader you can be a priority.

And in reminding you I remind myself that there is no magic to being a leader. It just requires making a conscious choice to make a positive difference.

You are now a part of the LeaderThink® family. Let us all be examples of leaders who are trustworthy, caring, courageous and fair.

Tracy Brown

About Tracy Brown

Tracy grew up in St. Louis, Missouri and attended public schools there. At school and at church she was expected to be a leader and to make a positive difference in the world. As a result, Tracy has achieved high goals in her profession and in her community.

She has served as a volunteer leader for more than a dozen community-based organizations involved in health care, the performing arts and improving life for previously homeless or disadvantaged individuals. She is one of the creators of the Dallas Dinner Table process, which brings people together in small groups to increase understanding about the impact of race and racism in the daily lives of local citizens. And she actively volunteers with the Center for Nonprofit Management helping leaders in agencies nationwide improve their ability to lead.

Tracy is President of Diversity Trends, LLC, a consulting and training firm based in Dallas, Texas. She helps her clients improve communication, leadership and customer service skills, strengthen their commitment to multicultural inclusion and align their people-focused programs with their strategic business priorities.

As an author and consultant Tracy has made appearances on many local radio and television programs. She's also been interviewed or featured nationally in Money Magazine, BLR Reports, The Network Journal, HR Insights, Texas Business Monthly, HR Magazine, Heart and Soul Magazine and other publications.

But Tracy is not all work and community service. Whatever city her business might take her to you can often find her relaxing at a rollerskating rink, or in the audience of a play or jazz concert.

LeaderThink® Email Newsletter

If you want to receive new LeaderThink® messages each Monday morning, subscribe to the email newsletter.

Visit the website: www.TheWayLeadersThink.com and complete the subscription box. Or, send an email to: Leaderthink-Subscribe@tracybrown.com

LeaderThink® Podcast
www.BlogTalkRadio.com/leaderthink

Listen or subscribe to the LEADERTHINK PODCAST to hear expanded versions of some of the most popular LeaderThink® messages!

Your Comments Are Welcome
If you have feedback about the book, let us know.

BY PHONE
Leave a voice message toll-free (in the U.S.) by calling 1.800.290.5631.

BY EMAIL
Send your comments or questions to: staff@TheWayLeadersThink.com

www.ingramcontent.com/pod-product-compliance
Lightning Source LLC
Chambersburg PA
CBHW071844200326
41519CB00016B/4236